or Tom
whose poems I
really liked.
love
Nolen
X

THE AFRICA
IN MY HOUSE

ANDREA MBARUSHIMANA

THE AFRICA IN MY HOUSE

ANDREA MBARUSHIMANA

Design by Hristo Dochev
Edited by Adam Steiner and Raef Boylan
All artwork by Andrea Mbarushimana

Published in the UK (2017)
by Silhouette Press
COVENTRY-LONDON
www.silhouettepress.co.uk
@SilhouettePress

DEDICATION

When it was suggested that I focus on my writing about Africa for my first collection, I was a bit uncomfortable about it and I still am. I didn't want to be just another *muzungu* (white foreigner) giving my white perspective on someone else's world.

I lived in Rwanda for two years. My experiences there and the relationships I made had a huge impact on me. For one thing, I came back married to a Rwandan. Our daughter is mixed-race and just beginning to identify as black. Writing is my way of laying down ideas, pulling threads and trying to work things out. I need to write about the Africa in my house. It's a journey that, for my daughter's sake, I'd like to share with you.

This book is dedicated to my beautiful husband and daughter and the rest of my African family (*ndabakunda cyane pe!*) and to all the African people who've been my teachers; from Maboyi, who used to wear half an old football as a hat and was the first person to make me feel welcome in Kigeme; to the friends and academics who've spent long hours talking to me about the complexities of culture and politics.

Thank you for your stories.

CONTENTS

HYENA

On the surface, some things always looked the same. The sunbirds suck nectar from the flowers at the side of the road, just as they always did. Old men still sit in seahorse hats with long sticks and suck sorghum beer from gourds through long straws. The potholes fill with dust and cough it out at the taxi-buses that dip and tilt, but the buses are not as full as they used to be.

It's been another day of nothing - sitting around having awkward conversations on dusty streets. A matter of looking for something, anything to do, trying to get used to the feel of other people's clothes, friends' clothes, not the usual ones that find their way in huge bails shipped over the ocean. These borrowed clothes itch with charity, stiffen my movements with self-consciousness, stimulate uncomfortable glances. My Hutu flat nose and my wide mouth type-cast me. I can see them wondering, 'Where was he? Is he a killer?'

Back at H's house, I am already anxious. I have to welcome whoever comes through that door as though they are a friend, knowing they might despise me, mock me, the sight of me might make them sick or fearful. I imagine the effort of a smile before I can summon one, manage to stretch my mouth into the right shape, dry lips taught over teeth. But when the door opens, for a second, I can't breathe. I never expected...and I close my eyes, briefly.

Back in the forest. We fell over each other, piling out of the lorry, stumbling towards the soldiers. Me, I'm trying to keep sight of Mum and P, desperate not to lose them again. Children are picked up off the ground. Babies cry, sensing panic. Line up! they order, more cackling, their spotted, camouflage jackets merging together into pelts. Single file! Our legs shake as the glucose-starved blood seeps back into them. Single file would stretch us out for miles over this sticky road, but it amused them to see us bow our woolly heads and try.

Oh, we were hilarious that day. I can see his friends laughing as he raises his muzzle towards us, they cackle and spit, their shoulders hunched and shivering. I can see light off his flashing teeth and feel the panic rumble and roll through my belly, a sudden sweat sending my lice into panic, writhing and biting, the skinless soles of my feet sweating blood and the heat of everyone around me. And that face, the cackling hyena face I saw then is in front of me now, in my friend's front room. The face of the hyena who pointed his gun at me, at my family, who threatened to kill us when we were already half dead.

My friend is introducing him to me and I rise from the wooden stool, as politeness requires, to embrace him with my rictus smile in place. His eyes are not the same. They have lost their glazed animal madness, but it is him and I am once again fearful of being eaten.

We talk. There are many things to talk about. I am careful not to touch on anything but banalities. When my friend leaves the room, my kind friend who has given me his roof, who feeds me food and offers me beer, the friend who I cannot disgrace, when he leaves, I say to the hyena before me: I know you. I have seen you before, in the forest. You threatened to shoot us.

He shudders, then barks a humourless laugh. The smell of eucalyptus smoke from a newly struck fire coils into the room. I examine him for signs of a predatory nature. He looks down at the wooden table and picks at the varnish with long fingernails. We are both champions at mastering ourselves for the sake of propriety.

He looks at me: Maybe it was me, he says. I was doing my job. If I hadn't done my job, well…you know how it is. I know. I have just come back from weeks spent digging up corpses in front of grieving relatives who blamed me for those deaths, people who didn't know me from the devil. It was not voluntary. I feel as though my fingernails, my hands will never be clean again. I am afraid to touch food with them.

I begin to see him as he really is: The stiffness of his limbs, his threadbare jacket, not much better than mine, the hollowness of his cheeks. In the bone structure of his face, I see the half-fleshed skulls I was forced to exhume for re-burial with a hoe. I wonder how either of us survived, but I never pointed a gun at anyone. I never hurt anyone. Thinking this, I begin to feel a little taller. I am standing on two feet. Perhaps I too am the last person in the world he wants to be with right now.

I ask him if he knows the Rwandan folk tale of Hyena and his shit. No, he tells me. Hyena's shit is white from crunching bones, so when he sees Cowpats on the ground, still steaming, he laughs to himself and says that politeness comes from the stomach. Because Hyena knows he is not polite. Because his shit is more polite than Cow's, who is revered. Because sometimes everyone must eat bones in order to survive and because Hyena knows himself and he knows Cow, too.

We look at each other and we are two people. I have nothing to fear from him.

LUCE

The women of my youth
Were careful and polished,
Nothing like you
With your proud flesh,
Solar smile.

Sensuality rippled off you,
Redolent with sex and sweat
You wore your children
Like orbiting moons,
Intimidated dignitaries with
Your Folk-hero's wit,
Ox strength.

How I loved you,
And swore to be all woman,
But here I am with my apologies
And etiquette,
My blunt razor and my gnawed pen.

You never learned how to be
Less than yourself.
I remember how it felt
When I first saw you.

MURAMBI GENOCIDE SITE

It's hard to find your way sometimes,
Past death's mask -
Along the broken path
Back to a life.

Through the classrooms of corpses, back
To the car, through the shrieking
Cicadae-d grass.

Closing my eyes, I see the yellow,
Blood-less, black-pored skin,
The flickering eyelashes,
Hear that last breath
And a line-up of bodies troops past,
Skulls stretched in silent screams.

I'm searching for a memory of your smile
But I can't see past the emptiness it left behind
Or the lesson of those classrooms,
The scars wearing the guide,
His family in room six.

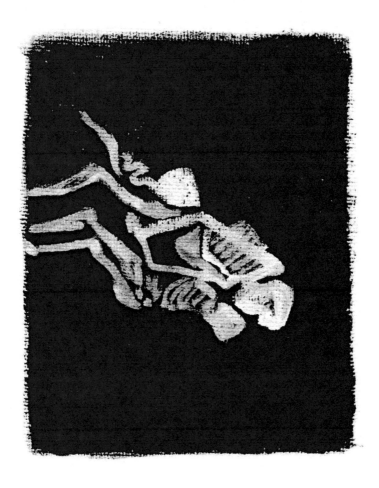

RABBIT

It's the rainy season, but now the clouds are gone. You can almost hear the water on the ground sizzle under the scouring sun. Red mud sucks at the house-boy's cracked toes. He's holding a rabbit by the ears, sawing at its throat with a blunt knife. The rabbit keens and writhes. An embarrassed smile splits the boy's face. There are two other people in the courtyard. A woman, skin white in the light reflecting off the concrete walls, complains:

"You're hurting it."

The woman comes over and takes the rabbit. She holds it around the neck, squeezing with both hands, telling herself that if she wants to eat meat, she should do this, should be able to kill for it. The rabbit kicks some more. It looks like someone's pet, she thinks: white fur peppered with black patches, like the shadow of a tree on concrete. A bird cracks off an alarm, which reverberates around the compound like gunfire. Mica crystals flash from the rabbit's fur as its kicking slows to a series of slow twitches.

It took less than a minute but felt longer. All she can think now is how easy it was. She gives the rabbit back to the boy and soon it is meat, flailed and ugly, all the softness gone.

You notice a fire in the corner. The stove is made from an old American Aid vegetable oil can: "Not for Sale or Exchange". It burns charcoal and a kindling of eucalyptus that flavours the smoke. Into a pan the carcass goes, over the heat. The man turns the meat, which spits and smokes. The woman talks to him in a low voice you can't quite hear. They lean through the smoke to kiss.

The house-boy's feet kick the ground, already dried to dust, toes picking up mica of their own, sparkling. The woman steps through the smoke, unfolds a note, hands it to the boy. He grins, it's a real grin this time and skips away, shrugging the patchy anorak from his bare, sinewed shoulders and shrugging it back again.

She thinks about the food in her mouth - tasteless and tough - and feels a strange numbness clinging to it. They leave nothing but the bones. Even the eyeballs are sucked-out.

SURVIVOR

We stood outside her house
And offered beer to her dead husband
Her family of cloud-limbed ghosts
Brushing our elbows.
"Don't tell me how to commemorate."
She muttered.
Her children knew that tone and kept away;
Four of them by different fathers.

I sometimes felt sorry for those
Helpless men when they visited,
Unsure if a particular child was theirs or not:
Powerful people reduced to
Sipping their longing through warm beer on the hard sofa.
She says:
You will not have these children for your conflicts,
They are MINE!

And folds her arms about me
Like gentle fingers rounding a white
Egg, her lips against my cheek.
As if I might crack
Under the weight of her anger,
The edges of her politics.

KIGEME

I
The crested eagle
Shivers his black crown and turns
Into the tree's breast

II
Behind the Pick-Up
Hangs in the quiet vacuum
The scent of red dust

III
A friend's memory
In the slow-curling vortex
Before the next rains

POWER CUTS, 2001

1 – RWANDA

Sudden dark and our students begin
Screeching and whooping,
We struggle to remember where we put the candles
Stumbling through the house
Finding each other's giggling faces;
Outside an irate owl shrieks at us.

The school generator whirs to life
And we follow its noise and light,
To the Staffroom
Where teachers congregate like moths.
Somebody drops a ruler.
"Doucement!" says a Congolese,
"Ce n'est pas la guerre!" and everybody laughs.
'Softly, this is not the war.'

We follow the owl back home.
And the scent that streams through the open door -
Angel's trumpets and Eucalyptus -
Eddies in dark corners.
The three of us sit and play with wax
As insects hiss and fizz in the candle flames.

II – U.K.

The reflection of our headlamps
Strokes the long-bellied, unlit streetlamps.
We can't buy petrol
Because the tills are down.
Apart from the panicked cashier
There's not a single soul.
Families sit, bereft of their TV sets
In the safety of other egg boxes.
The air is out of tune,
Thinly laced with diesel
And somewhere, in the darkness –
Rwanda's still at war in Congo.

REFUGEE ART GROUP

She goes in as they are folding up their bedding. The room is oppressive – the warmth of all the bodies from the night before taunts people who have to leave into the cold. Sometimes during the day she sees them sitting on benches in the park watching others, who can afford to give away their food, feeding the swans. Sometimes she meets them in the library browsing law books for their case or newspapers for news or directs them to the Jesus Army for breakfast and evangelism.

She gets the stuff out, the paints and paper and takes over the tables, gathers them round, asking them what the subject should be for today. They all agree – their favourite foods from home. Blank sheets transform into huge, shiny watermelon segments and complex dishes of rice. She's painting beans – Rose-Coco – huge, like monoliths of starch.

People talk about their problems and analyse their dreams. Some of them need to go to Solihull to sign, but for a while it's nice. They are here because they choose to be. They needn't draw if they don't want to. They can just make drinks and chill. But soon it's 11.00 and time to finish. They thank her and begin to leave, some making sandwiches to fill pockets that already carry most of the things they own; important papers torn and held together by string inside degrading plastic folders, the last letters they received from their families back home and identity cards they might get stopped and asked for.

One man's left in the room. He heard from his friend last night that another friend's been shot. He rubs the eyes they shone the lights into in that cell, the scars of burns visible on the backs of his hands and she hugs him as he shakes. Later on she sees him shouting at no-one in the Precinct, somewhere else and in some other time, pigeons flying round him. She calls to him and he's anchored by the familiar voice. She buys him coffee. It might do, for the next few hours.

HISTORY LESSON

Pixels, black and white, unknot and pool
Into shadow that crawls beneath
What might be a shoe,
Resolves into a foot,
In a puddle of blood.

I knew about the hands
The Belgians had a thing for lopping-off
Could you buy them once as souvenirs
On the streets of Brussels?
Ash trays.

There is a man turned away from the lens
Arms cradling himself.
The caption says 'father'
Can he hear the echo of his daughter
Cry amongst the leaves of the forest?
A cry he's known since birth?

He could go to her
But he can't take his eyes from the thing on the ground
The beautiful thing he's bathed in his rough hands.
The foot in the sand.
A foot that's hers.
A land that's hers.
Bleeding.

GATYAZO BAR

Luce is regal and rotund in her
Mobile-phone-print-wrap and
Dame Edna sunspecs.
She's spread out on the mat,
Grinning soft abuses at her customers,
Sour-breathed with home brew and gossip.

The seed heads cackle slowly in the heat,
Bee-Eaters flash, the heat cradles my head
Tension flows out of me like arpeggios
From a Congolese guitar.

Sometimes we'd move into the bar's back room.
Children rushed giggling through
The slats of dusty light
Trying to pluck our kisses from their eyes.

That was where I first said
I'd be proud to be your wife.

MUZUNGU

Porn-star/lottery-win-white-girl
Sits in the African staffroom
And muses why pale is still considered best
As she fields unasked-for advances
In a strange language,
Fields ire-filled glances
From local women.
And thinks: if I was raised like them
On porn-star/patronising/
Un-stained-by-sin/lottery-win-white-girls
I would hate me too.

Porn-star/lottery-win-white-girl
Sits in the corner
With her African tea (Nido!)
So sugary it makes her teeth hurt
And tries to smile politely.
When a new teacher arrives,
He says hello and shakes her hand
Then turns around.
She is so grateful to be normalised
He has her complete attention.

Public-enemy-white-girl becomes teacher-nicknamed-Rasta-white-girl
Because she tries to be nice to everyone
Beyond social convention,
It is a victory of sorts.

Anti-Cinderella-white-girl marries Rwandan-teacher
In a ceremony to which the whole village is invited and they all come
Speeches are made, goats are eaten, beer is drunk.
They don't call her *Muzungu* anymore.

It's hard leaving Rwandan family and friends.
People who survived and saw under her skin
And past her early, unthinking racism.
She brings her husband home to England.

Middle-class-white-girl (which at least is true) walks her baby in the park
And realises that with her brown-girl-in-the-pram
She is now trashy/easy/benefits-class-white-girl
She is nigger-loving-traitor-white-girl
Fields poison-dripping words and burning glances and sometimes even
hurled bananas.

Too white for you? Not quite white enough?

You can think about her what you like
She'll still live happily ever after
Just don't try telling her
Colonialism's dead.

TALES FROM THE STICKS

I

We were walking back from the bar Mum and her friend owned, along a wide, dusty, potholed avenue in the vacuum black, moonless night. The only light was coming from the Milky Way above and from the bushes in people's gardens, where a thousand glow-bugs prayed for love. Staggering along the road, giggling like idiots we stumbled when my torch went out. Every now and then I thought I could see someone – a deeper kind of darkness passing us in the night, but no one said "hello".

In the 80s a new drink came on the scene, distilled from pineapples. There are plenty of pineapples in Nyaruteja – it's famous for them – so there was plenty of this stuff to go around. Pretty soon they started calling it 'Yewe muntu' – ('Hey, you!') because people who drank it used to greet trees on the way home as if they were people and go up and hug them. One man, walking along the same avenue we were, got really angry that this tree wouldn't greet him back.

"Hey you!" he said. No response.

"Hey, I said hello, friend. How are you?"

But the tree stood mute and still. In a country where everyone greets everyone, effusively and in detail – the tree's behaviour was simply not acceptable. So the man got cross. He threw a punch, which splintered painfully against a branch. Shaking and humiliated, the man continued to try to fight the tree. Needless to say, the tree won. After that, 'Yewe muntu' kind of lost its popularity.

II

When I visited Nyaruteja the first time I was struck by its frontier-town atmosphere. I noticed that people who sold brochettes – barbecued meat on skewers – by the side of the road, always left the goat heads on. Apparently this is because, one time, someone discovered that they had eaten a dog kebab.

III

Because Nyaruteja is a long way from the capital, near the border with Burundi, it is out of the way in terms of policing and justice systems. Not so long ago, people used to take the law into their own hands, taking what was left to the police station, pre-judged. My husband remembers from his childhood, a sorry figure being dragged to the cells at the end of a long, painful drought; the rich red mud licking his bloody legs as he was frog-marched through the puddles. He was the local Rain-Maker. He'd been approached by townsfolk asking him to make it rain and time after time he'd tried to send them away to get more and yet more money. Because of the drought, no one had money that time. People were starving, desiccated, barely surviving. The townspeople lost their composure at his greed and beat him up. That very night, the rain fell, the drought breaking like a dam. After that – no rain maker was ever seen in Nyaruteja again: The people had worked out that beating up Rainmakers was the only sure way to get them to work properly.

THE HUMAN ANIMAL

Strawberry stained faces
Conversation foaming
She tells me proudly, how
Settling in Uganda,
She set up a charity for animals.
Those poor puppies.

I too have seen orphaned creatures snap at fingers for food
Sniff from bags on street corners
Weeping around their flies.

Mary Ellen, in 1872,
Was removed from abusive parents
Under a law against cruelty to animals.

Look how far we've come!
Cream puffed, Proseccoed,
Protecting white children
And African dogs.

HEALING

The first time you saw fireworks,
Fiery chemical blooms
Lit by their own smoke
I watched you regress, back to the camp:
Running from shells exploding with laval yolk,
Cracking the sky.

When we talk about visiting Rwanda our daughter's eyes light up
But she'll see her first grave there and what else?
Memorials and scars,
And what it might mean to be half-African, half-white.

What's the worth of a picked-over, pick and choose
Heritage I wonder?
How much to tell her about colonialism, slavery, genocide?
But watching her bright laugh at the big display
And new joy lighting up
Her father's face, I think:
Not yet,
Give us just a little more time.

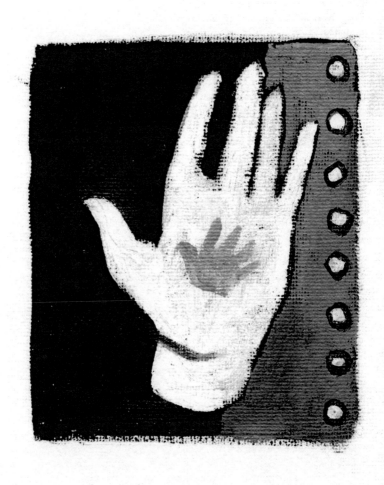

BROTHER!

They find each other in the street,
begin to laugh and snap their fingers,
panting memories of pitted dust.
I smile with them
as they converge with long strides.
Kisses dust cheeks,
contentment sighing through
louche, entangled limbs.

Foreign leaves fall towards them:
autumn confetti.
Ay-ay-ay-ay-ay
Eh-eh-eh-eh-eh!
They turn away from me,
little fingers of opposing hands
twisted together.
One turns to whisper to the other.

They're new, I guess.
Soon they'll unlearn their language of tenderness:
the sparks between them will fizzle out
into self-consciousness,
and the cold and the concrete
will set hard around their souls.
They will forget how to love each other.

TRANSACTIONS

It sits in his palm
A full stop of lead
Globular, dead and unreflective.
I take it, wonder if it's radioactive
Then guess:
Coltan?

I read about this -
Carving up the forest
Chewing up the people
And spitting them out.
Feeding the hunger of the digital generations:
Granny had her diamonds,
Grandad his gold,
Now we have our phones, our iPads.
In Congo the cost is measured in lost childhoods.

He's proud of it.
Look! Look what I have!
He thinks it'll make him rich.
But he's a sorry looter of other people's dreams
He looks at me like I am his white queen.
Take it and go, I think
But privilege confers a dark heart
No matter how hard you try
To stay clean.

NEIGHBOURHOOD KIDS

I showed you a photo of some kids I knew.
You described it back to me:
A picture of brown, African children
Kwashiorkor bellies distended under ragged
T-shirts stained with dirt
In adult jeans cut short to fit their tiny legs
Big brown eyes and naked feet.
"Poor kids," you said.

And in my shock. I forgot their names,
The games my husband played with them
The screams of their delight
And felt as though you'd taken out my eyes
Replacing them with TV screens.

REGRESSION

That year the rains didn't come
It was the last, bad joke.
I worked the thirsty, cracked earth
'Till I bled into it my most bitter bile,
Frustration threatening to make the crops taste bad,
Sweat was poison to the soil.

While others cackled,
Mocked this teacher's son,
A student all my life
Subsisting on air and sweat
Shedding all his fat promises
Growing muscles like tumours.

But we turned those dead fields around,
Bananas, leaves peeled back, shot up
Tumescent in their approval.
And when the rains finally came
I spilled the last of my promise out
Dancing in zombie ecstasy,
Writhing in mud
Became a squirming termite.

FOLK TALE RESURRECTION

Another friend gone.
Africa keeps eating
Pieces of me.
Lightning bolts fall
From the lips of soft clouds.
Picking their teeth with my loss.

If I give all of myself
Perhaps I can be coughed
Back up like Muguru
(without my heart?)
Listening to the excuses of talking dogs.

Maybe in the belly of Africa
Is where I belong
With all the friends I've lost
To her insatiable appetite.
If only they could be
Disgorged,
Gasping, enslimed, but somehow still alive
Like in the stories.

DINNER

Preparing for the feast
Can you taste home in the food?
If not, it wasn't done right.
Everything is chopped straight into the pot
The kids run, trailing random tasks like kites,
Who is the big man here?
The women are all big:
Big jokes,
Big hearts,
Big partiers,
Big movers,
Joking on their men
Who stutter over speeches
And swoon over sauces,
Loving to love them.

GOD OF SHADOWS

The room is a dense, pulsing, blue-green. In the low light it is like being under a thick canopy of leaves. There are pictures of the Virgin Mary round the room and one of Jennifer Lopez. A single mattress on the floor, covered with sheets and many-coloured blankets, is hooded by a mosquito net, knotted and swinging. There is a small set of drawers in the corner and on the floor are a couple of cardboard boxes with books and papers inside. Clothes and things belonging to two girls are folded on the drawers, but Marie is still at school, far away. Could she help if she was here?

The single, small window with a ragged curtain in front of it, is a little open. Here are the things you can hear: The afternoon rain, drumming on the roof, on all the rooves of the neighbourhood; the water running in rivers down the street and a group of girls who got caught in the rain and became so wet in the first ten seconds it was not worth going inside. They play, sing and laugh, jump in puddles and dance. Water, salt water runs down the face of the girl inside who is listening to them from the small, grubby mattress. Constance, Conny, keeps up a litany of her own to match the drumming on the rooves. If you got closer you would hear she is praying. She is praying to bleed.

No sex out of marriage, the American Pastor had said. He kept saying it: No sex. No sex. The more he said it the more she thought about it, the more powerful it became. Conny saw the way the Pastor's eyes flamed as he said the words, the way he agitated and sweated. She could see Pascal out of the corner of her eye as she listened. She could imagine the scent of his neck.

A week passes. Conny will not leave her room and her family is worried. She tries to tell them, but she has let them down so badly, she can't find the words. All the sweat they poured into getting her an education has dried into salt. Her small breasts feel like rocks that have been stapled to her chest through the skin. She sobs and shivers and will not talk to anyone. Her tongue swells with praying. It's not working! Why would God listen to her? She thinks about the children of the American Pastor.

He lined all nine of them up on the stage to receive praise and you could tell God loved them; their eyes shined with their confidence in God's blessing and they were strong and beautiful and pale, with gold hair like haloes in the stadium lights. The boys all looked like Jesus – Jesus in the posters framed in her parents' living room, the posters in her school room, the paintings in her church.

Conny buries her head in the covers. These thoughts are not helping her. There must be something she hasn't tried. Being white enough? What a joke! Her chest heaves. "Keep the light of God within you!" There is more than light inside her now. She doesn't want it. She is afraid. There is something at the edge of her mind. Something she should remember... Maybe it is OK for the white people to pray in their way, but maybe their way isn't working for her because she is isn't white? Maybe she needs to find another way to pray. And she remembers: Her sister once had something else inside her too. She misses Marie so much. A God of Light is also a God of shadows.

Conny has to see what's happening and she's pushing through the crowd of sweaty bodies into the space by the wall of her house, to see her sister. Baby girl she begs, Marie, please be OK. But Marie is so still, so grey and slippery. They have tried every medicine the Pharmacist suggested and nothing, no improvement. For days Conny has not been allowed to even touch her sister. She's sung her throat dry from the next room to let Marie know how she's loved. Everyone else spends the night together in there now, in the only other bedroom in the house: a sleepless tangle, listening to Marie wheezing from behind the thin wall.

This morning her sister was carried outside by their father, barely breathing. People jostle Conny from behind. Papa sees her and comes to stand beside her, making it clear that, although he will not shoo anyone away, their presence is barely tolerated.

The Medicine Man crouches over Marie. He takes a knife. Conny surges forward, but Papa's strong arms fold around her and she sniffs and shakes against them. It's OK, Cowbell, he says in his deep voice. (That was what he used to call her, her baby name). It'll be OK, he says. The Medicine Man moves the knife slowly across the shadow of her sister's stomach. Marie sighs through her fever. The crowd gasps. He takes another instrument, like scissors, but with long, flattened noses like spoonbill beaks. He reaches towards Marie's shadow and dips the spoonbill-scissors into it, in the same place he made the cut and with his face screwed up like the shrivelling, puckered skin of an old passion fruit, he pulls. Marie's shadow moves with the spoonbill scissors, changing shape, pulling upwards.

The crowd holds their collective breath. Then something breaks. They gasp! The Medicine Man grunts as he pulls something from the shadow of Conny's sister, through her shadow stomach – a pulsing, separate shadow – a living shadow thing, like a huge, fat worm coming out of her shadow body. Marie cries out as it leaves her and there are two shadows on the wall, hers and the thing in the scissors.

Conny loses track of things, buried in her Papa's arms. Mama is with Marie, back in the house. People leave. The Medicine Man is talking to Papa. Marie is awake and speaking coherently for the first time in weeks. Conny should be with her, wants to be, but she's afraid of what she saw, remembers the shadow thing that came out of her sister. What happened to it? She panics, searching for it with her eyes across the compound, in her mind, it takes the shape of the gecko she sees in the toilet block, the one that's flecked with brown, the one that Isa told her God fashioned from toenail clippings. The gecko is horrible when she can see it, glaring at her with its sorghum-red snake-eyes from the roof, but worse when she can't see it, when she doesn't know where it is. Where did the shadow go? Is it slithering invisibly across the ground towards her, looking for another body to poison? Papa can feel the panic in her. He lifts Conny up.

"It's OK. She's going to be OK."
"But where is the thing, Papa?"
"Oh!" He laughs.
"It died. It died. It won't bother us anymore." He looks for confirmation at the Medicine Man, who looks at Conny and grins, his mouth lined with brown, rotted teeth. In that moment, Conny is more afraid of the man than the shadow thing.

In the dead of night, when everyone sleeps, Conny creeps outside and collects a knife and a candle from the place where they cook. Are there any other choices? There is only one way she could get the money she would need and there would be no going back from that – she could catch something worse than a child. There is no way she would ask Pascal or his family. They are struggling as much as her own.

For a moment she looks up at the sky, clear now, at the rich vein of stars that wanders through it. She can hear insects and smell toothpaste spat on the ground and the flowers from the tree near the latrine. Her hand moves over her stomach and she begins to cry again. She takes the knife and the candle back into the room, lies on the bed on her back and places the candle, which she lights with a match, to one side. She feels a little foolish, but her flickering hope is more painful than her fear now. She has to try. Conny wriggles till she gets in the right position to see the shadow of her stomach thrown against the green wall and sniffs her tears back.

Lying in the pocket of light, she can't remember what the Medicine Man said, but she appeals to her ancestors through the spirit of Ryangombe. Her words trip and spill over each other and jumble and blur and eventually, she invokes a kind of hysteria, a kind of trance. The candle is burning down. An owl screeches outside and she jerks, half awake. She takes the knife to the shadow of her belly and cuts.

OUT OF WATER (1999)

The air is full of
Tupac, Christina Aguilera, Wenga Musica from
Bootleggers on every corner.
Toothbrush, tissue and biscuit sellers,
Silk-mouthed contenders,
Competing for the cash of
Congolese shiny patterned shirts
Flashing in shoals and
Ladies day-glo-green netted shoulders
Topping voluminous dresses.
A reef of colours more various than
English adjectives
Slides and weaves across my vision.
The air is stuffed with clashing odours
Cat-fish from Victoria sway their stinking whiskers,
Fronded, pocked and brain-ridged fruit
Savage the senses.
Tattered kids on their twelve-hour-tired feet
Offer peanuts to hermetically-sealed bus windows
Business suits undulate their gleaming, ample inches.
And then there's me,
Sunburnt in shabby denim,
My mouth opening and closing at everything.

INKA

Inka are cows and also game-pieces. Cows are important; they have their own songs, their own colours and the giving of cows represents the joining of people and families. Cows are used as dowry, they are given to cement relationships – friendships, or relationships of patronage. So when I decided to give Gasarenda a cow, it was a big deal. The trouble was, I didn't have a cow to give.

Since the genocide and the war, we had been running. We had taken only the most important things for survival: cooking pans and blankets, that sort of thing. I had been a student and I loved reading. I couldn't flee without taking at least one book. The book I had chosen was a dog-eared copy of Victor Hugo's 'Les Miserables', the only personal item I had with me. It would be painful to part with – a good cow – I hoped Gasarenda would like it.

I remember the day I first met him. He was sat in the back of one of the language classes I taught in our makeshift school in the refugee camp. Some people, who had no interest in languages at all, came to the school just for something to do. It felt useful, more useful than just sitting around or fucking – there were not many other options.

Gasarenda was different. Pretty soon I discovered that he was able to speak English easily, as proficiently as me, the teacher. I asked around and heard he was an ex-officer from the Rwandan army, who'd left a while before the genocide started. We began to chat now and again and soon became friends. He worked in the camp for a German Aid Agency, a very well-paid job for a refugee. What's more, he was in charge of firewood – that was a big deal.

After working at the school I would go back to my blue, plastic UNHCR-sheeting tent, to rot for a bit in the damp heat. Later, I would go to my Mum's tent to eat with her and my little brother. We charged one dollar a term, per person at the language school and Mum was good at making my share of the school fees go a long way, eking the money out into something that could sustain me, my little brother, our cousin and herself. I gave her my wages to buy food - a little flour, a few beans, from people in the camp who needed cash for other things, like soap, or a knife – and when she had enough, she took the produce to the market to sell to local Congolese.

The food we refugees were given, in contrast to the sticky atmosphere, was desiccated almost beyond recognition; dry beans, maize husks hard as bullets, maize flour, dried lentils, a series of full stops. The Aid Agencies handed out one can of each to everyone and each can was supposed to last a week. You might wonder where we could possibly get the water to cook all this dried produce. We were left wondering that, too, sometimes. And where did we get the firewood to cook all this stuff for long enough to make it soft enough to go down?

Survival, along with politics, dominated every conversation. There were times we would go without being given any firewood at all, for a week, sometimes longer. Everyone helped each other and we got by somehow, but it was tough. Once I knew Gasarenda, we were alright in that regard. He made sure we had enough firewood, sneaking us an extra log or two. In addition to that, he sometimes bought me beer. Being able to go to the tent-bar and drink beer, relax and chat, made a big difference to me. It took me out of the situation we were in, my worries about survival, everything.

So, I devised a plan to give to Gasarenda my cow. The day I chose for the ceremony we were drinking in the tent-bar, our usual meeting place; a wooden frame, like everything, covered with the same blue, plastic sheets, making a room about ten by five metres. The walls were ingeniously punctuated by refugee-crafted, wooden-framed, blue-sheeted windows which could be opened and closed. Light cut through them, razoring blue shadows into segments which pooled together on the dirt floor. People were drinking urwagwa – banana beer – a sour and grainy brew, which back home was only really drunk by the poorest people, alcoholics and old men with long sticks and a penchant for cowboy hats. Here in the camp, only a few lucky ones like Gasarenda could afford bottled lager. I was incredibly nervous when I stood and began my speech. The room fell silent, listening to me, well used to the traditional etiquette of speeches, but words which were alien to this strange, blue outpost of displaced Rwandan culture. I had never been in any kind of ceremony where a cow had been replaced by something else. Would Gasarenda understand? I felt the sweat run down my back as I explained that the cow used to have an ornate earring, which had been torn out – in order to explain a few torn and missing pages from my book. When I finished, there were claps and shouts and Gasarenda, to my huge relief, was grinning at me in delight. He made a return speech thanking me.

"This cow is gratefully and humbly accepted. Its body is thick and firm." He gestured to the depth of the book and hefted it in his hands to show the crowd its weight. Laughter shook the thin walls of the tent.

"Its torn ear is an imperfection that draws attention to the perfection of the remaining form. Its character is charming and full of depth. The giver of this cow is a particular friend who I am very fortunate to know. To meet such a thoughtful, generous and sophisticated person has brought me great pleasure." Everyone cheered! The speeches and drinking continued into the night.

I thought that was the end of it. I was pleased Gasarenda liked his cow; I'd given it to him earnestly, not as a joke, but I knew my tattered book was a poor substitute for an actual cow. Then, a few months later, he came to me one day and said:

"Do you remember asking me for the time, the other day? Don't ever do that again!"

And, laughing, he handed me a watch: a stainless steel analogue watch that actually wound up. How had he noticed my love of watches? It was a sign of brotherhood and I was speechless with emotion. I remember it had a beautiful blue dial. I had never owned a watch before in my entire life. I loved it. I understood that Gasarenda had given me a cow in return.

We knew there was a war going on and every day it got closer. People began to arrive at the camp having fled from other camps, further into the country, which had been attacked. We heard that the rebels were in Bukavu City, only thirty kilometres away. Then one morning, with no warning and no preparation, the aid agencies didn't appear at the camp. They'd left their fancy hotels and fled back to their own countries, leaving us between the closing jaws of the oncoming armies. We had become totally dependent on their handouts of food and their protection and suddenly we were on our own – tens of thousands of people with nothing to eat. Our school stopped. We lived, somehow, for another month on the scraps that people had managed to save (from pretending they had more children than they actually did, for example). Some people began working, doing odd jobs for local Congolese people for food. Mum's surplus stock kept us going. We ate a handful-sized meal in the middle of each day. I remember going three or four times to an area that had been cleared of trees, to try to cut and scrape out the leftover stumps for firewood, blisters ballooning and popping all over my hands as I worked our borrowed axe back and forth, bleeding into the wood.

On the second of November, a Saturday morning, the rumours sharpened into the whistles of bullets. People started fleeing everywhere in chaos. A vehicle drove through the camp out of which a soldier shouted to us that a mortar was about to be launched by their side against the other and not to worry. When the mortar did go off I forgot everything they'd said. The explosion reverberated through my whole body, leaving me trembling, my stomach liquid. I dived to the ground instinctively. Panicking, desperate to get away, when the noise stopped I ran in one direction, not knowing my family was running in another.

After painful weeks of being apart, Christmas that year found us all together again under a bush in the middle of the rainforest, gunfire all around us, having eaten only a few peanuts in the last five days. When the shooting stopped we put on the small radio I had, hoping to get some news of the peril we were in. We didn't know it was Christmas day until then. The Voice of America station was filled with carols and talk of Santa or Father Christmas – the first I'd ever heard of him. After a few minutes of the DJs describing their presents and the feasts everyone would be eating, we turned it off.

For months we stumbled through the forest, becoming an increasingly ragged band: Muddied, bleeding from our raw feet; afro-ed and starving while eaten alive by lice, people wore all the clothes they owned to avoid them being lost or stolen. We were with a big group of refugees by then – thousands of us. Asked our destination we always replied 'the road' – the road to somewhere else, or a paved road, which would mean the end of our journey, one way or another – since the armies used the roads to move around.

I looked at my cow regularly, by now nostalgic even for the refugee camp, wondering what had happened to my friend. Day after day in the forest was killing us. No one had any food that wasn't found growing wild, or in the fields of Congolese who had fled. We were at the very edge of survival. One day, when a Congolese man appeared with some fish he had caught in a nearby lake, I knew it was time for the cow I'd been given to be slaughtered: I sold the watch for those fish.

Looking back, there is no doubt in my mind that the fish saved our lives.

We wept as we savoured it: silver-whiskered cow-book-watch-fish. It was a turning point. After that, it became easy to sell everything. The trousers I'd been wearing, one pair over the other, shirts off my back. Somehow we found enough to keep going. It was a month before we met the paved road and eventually made it home to Rwanda. More than a year later, in a taxi bus travelling through the capital city, I saw someone who looked just like Gasarenda, flashing past the window. I couldn't be sure, but I hope it was him, that he too survived. He was carrying a book under his arm. A fat book, full of promise.

Andrea Mbarushimana is a community worker, artist and writer. Andrea has been published in the London Magazine and Here Comes Everyone, exhibited in the Herbert Art Gallery and Museum, Coventry Cathedral Chapel of Unity and on various brick walls and has worked with refugees, minority groups, young people and parents.

Andrea made two short films televised on the Community Channel, one with young migrants and one tackling Islamophobia and she's a regular spoken word performer at Fire and Dust in Coventry. Her Uncle once described her as 'a real searcher', which feels about right.

Friends Of Palestine Poetry competition winner
Inshuti Friend exhibition at the Herbert (graphic short story)
Uncovering Coventry Culture exhibition funded by Coventry21 - poetry and blog

The poem Brother! was first published by the Algebra of Owls.

Twitter - @andymba24
www.andrea-mbarushimana.com